Tigers

Victoria Blakemore

vblakemore.author@gmail.com

Copyright info/picture credits

Cover, Pexels/Pixabay; Page 3, Pexels/Pixabay; Page 5, SusuMa/Pixabay; Page 7, Hamelin/Pixabay; Page 9, stafichukanatoly/Pixabay; Pages 10-11, Nawalescape/Pixabay; Page 13, Alexas_Fotos/Pixabay; Page 15, Innersanity/Pixabay; Page 17, Alexas_Fotos/Pixabay; Page 19, Pexels/Pixabay; Page 21, Sarah Cheriton-Jones/AdobeStock; Page 23; Pexels/Pixabay; Page 25, Joachim_Marian_Winkler/Pixabay; Page 27, WGRIECO/Pixabay; Page 29, Pexels/Pixabay; Page 31, Pixelmixer/Pixabay; Page 33, Alexas_Fotos/Pixabay

Table of Contents

What Are Tigers?

Tigers are large mammals.

They are the largest

members of the cat family.

Most tigers are orange with

black stripes. They can also

be black with tan stripes or

white with black stripes.

A tiger's stripes are like human fingerprints. No two tigers have the same stripes.

Kinds of Tigers

There are six kinds of tigers left in the wild. They differ in size, color, and where they live.

The Siberian tiger is the largest kind of tiger. They can weigh up to 660 pounds.

Bengal tigers sometimes

have white fur with black

stripes.

Physical Characteristics

Tigers have large paws with sharp claws. They use their claws to catch and eat their prey.

Tigers have back legs that are longer than their front legs. This helps them to jump as far as ten feet in one leap.

Habitat

Tigers are found in many different habitats. They live in forests, grasslands, marshes, rainforests, and the **taiga**.

Their stripes work as **camouflage**. They help tigers to blend in with trees and grasses.

Range

Tigers are only found on the continent of Asia.

Many are found in Thailand, India, China, Russia, and a few other countries.

Diet

Tigers are carnivores, which means that they eat meat. They have been known to eat over eighty pounds in one meal.

Their diet is made up of deer, wild pigs, antelope, yaks, and other animals.

Tigers are good hunters. They hide and wait to jump out and catch their prey.

Tigers do most of their hunting at night. The darkness helps them to hide from prey they are hunting.

Unlike some other big cats, tigers hunt alone. They do not work in groups to catch prey.

Tigers are **nocturnal**. They are active at night. This makes it easy for them to sneak up on their prey.

Communication

Tigers use different sounds to communicate. They can roar, grunt, and hiss. Sounds may be a greeting, a sign of danger, or a warning to stay away.

Tigers mark their **territory** with a special scent. It lets other tigers know to stay away.

Tigers are one of the few

big cats that can roar.

Movement

Tigers can run up to forty miles per hour. They can only run this fast for short distances.

Tigers are able to travel long distances. They regularly **patrol** their territory looking for food.

Tigers are good swimmers. They can swim across rivers.

Tiger Cubs

Tigers can have up to seven babies, which are called cubs. Most tigers do not have more than two cubs.

Mothers protect cubs from **predators** and teach them how to hunt. Tiger cubs stay with their mother for about two years.

Tiger cubs are very playful.

They wrestle, chase, and

play-fight with each other.

Solitary Life

Tigers are **solitary** animals.

They spend most of their

time alone.

Tigers are very **territorial**.

They do not like other tigers

to be in their area. Tigers

roam their territory and may

fight any other tigers they

find there.

Tigers do not like to share their territory. They like their own space to hunt.

Lifespan

In the wild, tigers usually live between ten and fifteen years.

In **captivity**, tigers may live longer. The oldest tiger on record was in a zoo in Australia. The tiger lived for twenty-six years.

Population

Tigers are **endangered**. There are not many left in the wild. There used to be nine species of tigers, but three are **extinct**.

In 2015, there were less than 4,000 tigers left in the wild. Tiger populations in the wild are still **declining**.

There are no more South

Chinese tigers left in the wild.

There are only a few left in zoos.

Tigers in Trouble

Tigers have been hunted by people for many years. In some places, they have been hunted because people think they are pests.

Some people use parts of tigers, such as teeth and bones, to make medicine.

Hunting and habitat loss are the two main threats facing wild tigers today.

Helping Tigers

Many countries have laws that prevent people from hunting tigers. They are also not allowed to be taken from the wild for sale.

Other countries do not allow people to sell things made with tiger teeth or bones.

Groups around the world

are working to protect

tiger habitats.

Some countries have set

up **preserves** where tigers

live and are protected.

People are not allowed to

build on this land or harm

tigers that live there.

Glossary

Camouflage: using color to blend in to the surroundings

Carnivore: an animal that eats only meat

Captivity: animals that are kept by humans, not in the wild

Declining: getting smaller

Endangered: at risk of becoming extinct

Extinct: when there are no more of an animal left in the wild

Nocturnal: animals that are active and night

Patrol: to guard by taking regular trips through

Predator: an animal that hunts other animals for food

Preserves: areas of land set up to protect plants and animals

Solitary: living alone

Taiga: forested land that is near the Arctic

Territorial: when an animal is protective of its territory

Territory: an area of land that an animal claims as its own

About the Author

Victoria Blakemore is a first grade
teacher in Southwest Florida with a
passion for reading.

You can visit her at

www.elementaryexplorers.com

Also in This Series

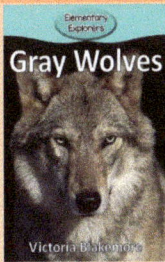

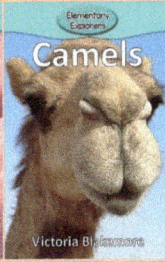

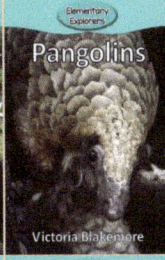

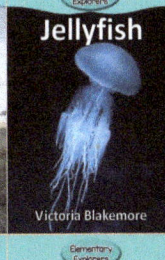

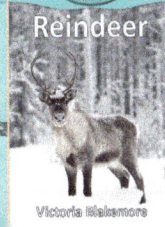

Elementary Explorers **Gray Wolves** Victoria Blakemore	Elementary Explorers **Sloths** Victoria Blakemore	Elementary Explorers **Flamingos** Victoria Blakemore	Elementary Explorers **Camels** Victoria Blakemore	Elementary Explorers **Koalas** Victoria Blakemore	Elementary Explorers **Honey Bees** Victoria Blakemore
Elementary Explorers **Pandas** Victoria Blakemore	Elementary Explorers **Pangolins** Victoria Blakemore	Elementary Explorers **White-Tailed Deer** Victoria Blakemore	Elementary Explorers **Orcas** Victoria Blakemore	Elementary Explorers **Giraffes** Victoria Blakemore	Elementary Explorers **Corn** Victoria Blakemore
Elementary Explorers **Meerkats** Victoria Blakemore	Elementary Explorers **Echidnas** Victoria Blakemore	Elementary Explorers **Walruses** Victoria Blakemore	Elementary Explorers **Raccoons** Victoria Blakemore	Elementary Explorers **Bald Eagles** Victoria Blakemore	Elementary Explorers **Apples** Victoria Blakemore
Elementary Explorers **Arctic Foxes** Victoria Blakemore	Elementary Explorers **Red Pandas** Victoria Blakemore	Elementary Explorers **Cassowaries** Victoria Blakemore	Elementary Explorers **Tigers** Victoria Blakemore	Elementary Explorers **Ladybugs** Victoria Blakemore	Elementary Explorers **Moose** Victoria Blakemore
Elementary Explorers **Beluga Whales** Victoria Blakemore	Elementary Explorers **Leopards** Victoria Blakemore	Elementary Explorers **Elephants** Victoria Blakemore	Elementary Explorers **Jellyfish** Victoria Blakemore	Elementary Explorers **Binturongs** Victoria Blakemore	Elementary Explorers **Lions** Victoria Blakemore
Elementary Explorers **Dolphins** Victoria Blakemore	Elementary Explorers **Reindeer** Victoria Blakemore	Elementary Explorers **Hammerhead Sharks** Victoria Blakemore	Elementary Explorers **Hippos** Victoria Blakemore	Elementary Explorers **Pumpkins** Victoria Blakemore	Elementary Explorers **Peafowl** Victoria Blakemore

Also in This Series

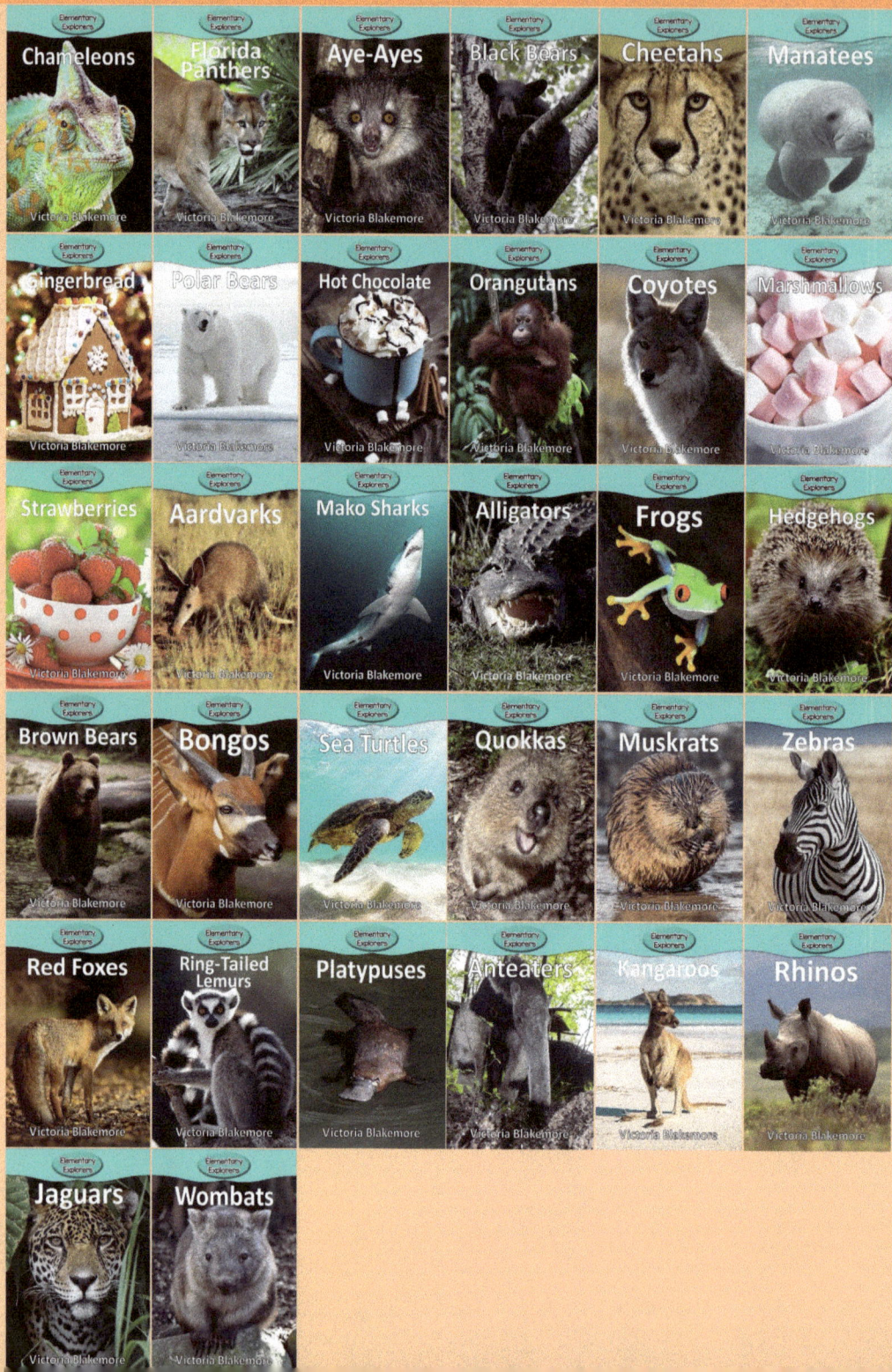

Chameleons	**Florida Panthers**	**Aye-Ayes**	**Black Bears**	**Cheetahs**	**Manatees**
Gingerbread	**Polar Bears**	**Hot Chocolate**	**Orangutans**	**Coyotes**	**Marshmallows**
Strawberries	**Aardvarks**	**Mako Sharks**	**Alligators**	**Frogs**	**Hedgehogs**
Brown Bears	**Bongos**	**Sea Turtles**	**Quokkas**	**Muskrats**	**Zebras**
Red Foxes	**Ring-Tailed Lemurs**	**Platypuses**	**Anteaters**	**Kangaroos**	**Rhinos**
Jaguars	**Wombats**				

All titles: Elementary Explorers — Victoria Blakemore

www.ingramcontent.com/pod-product-compliance
Lightning Source LLC
Chambersburg PA
CBHW051254020426
42333CB00025B/3203